ANCIENT CIVILIZATIONS AND THEIR MYTHS AND LEGENDS

ANCIENT EGYPTIAN CIVILIZATION

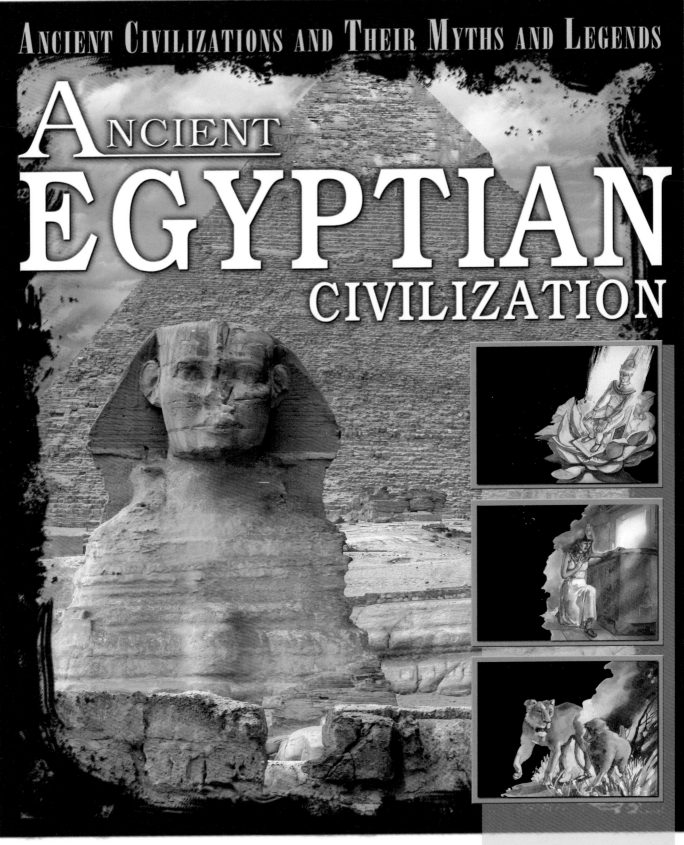

This edition published in 2010 by:

The Rosen Publishing Group, Inc.
29 East 21st Street
New York, NY 10010

Cover design by Nelson Sa.

Photo Credits: Cover, pp. 1, 3 © www.istockphoto.com/domin_domin; p. 24 (bottom left) Bildarchiv Preussischer Kulturbesitz/Art Resource, NY.

Library of Congress Cataloging-in-Publication Data

Bell, Michael, 1978–
Ancient Egyptian civilization / Michael Bell and Sarah Quie ; illustrations by Francesca D'Ottavi.
   p. cm.—(Ancient civilizations and their myths and legends)
Includes index.
ISBN-13: 978-1-4042-8034-2 (library binding)
1. Egypt—Civilization—To 332 B.C.—Juvenile literature. 2. Mythology, Egyptian—Juvenile literature. I. Quie, Sarah. II. D'Ottavi, Francesca, ill. III. Title.
DT61.B1455 2010
932—dc22

2009012361

Manufactured in the United States of America

Copyright © McRae Books, Florence, Italy.

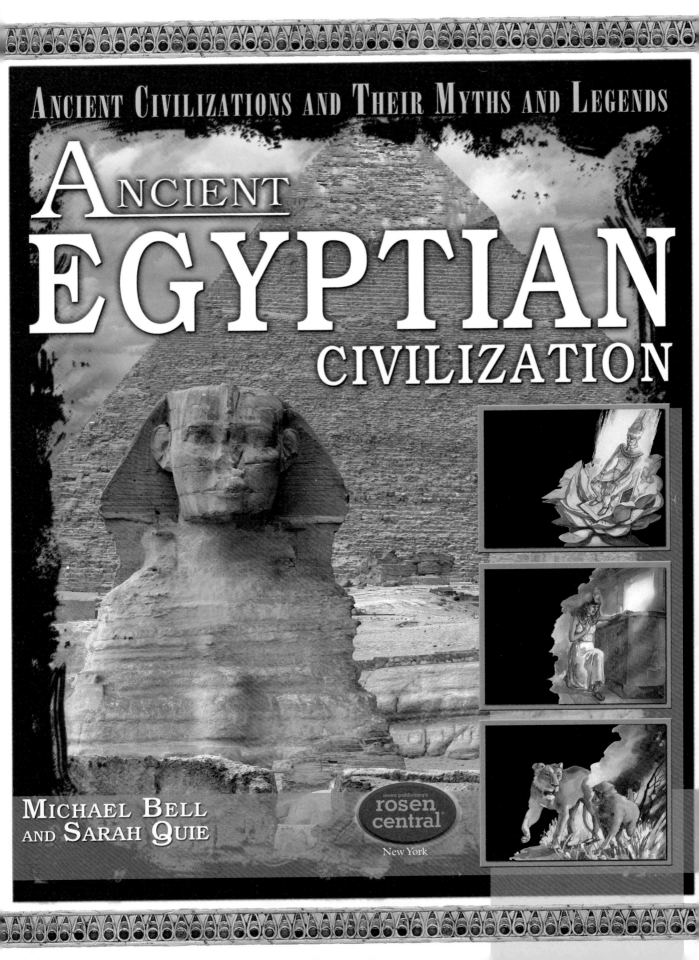

ANCIENT CIVILIZATIONS AND THEIR MYTHS AND LEGENDS

ANCIENT
EGYPTIAN
CIVILIZATION

MICHAEL BELL
AND SARAH QUIE

rosen publishing's
rosen central
New York

CONTENTS

INTRODUCTION 5
How this book works 5

THE CREATION 6
Geography and History 8

OSIRIS AND SETH 10
Egyptian Religion 12

AMUN-RA'S NIGHTLY JOURNEY 14
Burial Customs 16

THE BATTLE FOR KINGSHIP 18
The Pharaoh 20

THOTH BRINGS HATHOR BACK 22
The Scribe 24

THE BOATING PARTY 26
Women and Family Life 28

THE MAGICIAN 30
Food and Daily Life 32

THE SHIPWRECKED SAILOR'S TALE 34
Trade and Expansion 36

HOW THE BLESSED LIVED 38
Life along the Nile 40

Animals in Egyptian Society 42

Glossary 44
For More Information 45
For Further Reading 46
Index 47

INTRODUCTION

Ancient Egyptian civilization flourished along the banks of the River Nile for almost 3,000 years. It was one of the most brilliant and long-lasting civilizations in the ancient world. Even now, 2,000 years after it faded into the Greek and Roman empires, it continues to fascinate. The Egyptians left behind more traces of themselves than any other ancient civilization, and Egypt's very dry climate has preserved them through the centuries. The Sphinx and many of the pyramids, mummies, death masks, papyri, and tomb paintings are still visible today. The beauty and exotic nature of Egypt's material culture is explored in this book through simple texts and reproductions of artifacts and the retelling of Egyptian myths.

HOW THIS BOOK WORKS

This book is divided into sections. Each one starts with an Egyptian myth, strikingly illustrated on a black background. This is followed by a nonfiction spread about Egyptian society. The last section explores the strong links between Egyptian civilization and animals.

18

THE BATTLE FOR KINGSHIP

When Horus grew up he decided to challenge his wicked and cunning uncle Seth for the throne. Horus believed that, as the son of Osiris, he was the rightful ruler of Egypt. So he appealed to the gods, demanding that they make him pharaoh. But Seth was outraged, maintaining that as the strongest of all the gods he should be king.

After much discussion the gods decided to award Horus the throne. But Seth would not accept defeat and challenged Horus to a contest. Each god had to turn himself into a hippopotamus and remain submerged under the waters of the Nile. If either emerged within three months, he would lose the throne. But Isis, Horus's mother, feared for her son's safety. She was afraid that Seth would try to kill Horus under the water.

Isis threw a copper harpoon into the Nile, hoping to hit Seth. But it was Horus that leapt up. "Mother," he cried in pain, "you have hit me, your son!" Isis quickly withdrew her harpoon. Aiming once again she thrust it back into the Nile. This time she hit Seth. "Dearest sister," Seth cried cunningly, "do not hurt me, your brother." At this, Isis once again withdrew her harpoon.

As Isis had ruined the first contest Seth challenged Horus again. This time they were to race down the Nile in boats of stone. Now it was Horus's turn to be cunning. He knew that stone could not float. So he built a wooden boat and covered it with limestone to make it look like stone. Seth foolishly made his boat out of a mountain peak, which sank as soon as it hit the water. Seth was furious. How dare Horus trick him! Angrily Seth transformed himself into a hippopotamus and attacked Horus's boat.

Desperate to end the fighting between Horus and Seth, the gods finally turned to Osiris for advice. Osiris insisted that his son Horus was the rightful king and threatened to order savages from the Underworld to eat the gods' hearts if they did not respect his wishes. Fearing Osiris's wrath the gods immediately crowned Horus as the pharaoh of all Egypt.

19

Spread with myth of the battle for kingship leads on to a nonfiction spread on the importance of the pharaoh in Egyptian society.

In this book we explore Egypt's mythology and its civilization. By combining the two, we show how knowledge of mythology provides the basis for understanding Egyptian society. Religion was a very important part of Egyptian culture, and to explain why the Egyptians believed what they did, or behaved as they did, we must turn to their mythology. It helps to explain why Egyptians had such elaborate and costly funerary customs, such as building pyramids, making mummies and preparing burial goods. Through their mythology, we begin to understand why the Egyptians accepted and obeyed the pharaoh as supreme ruler of their country.

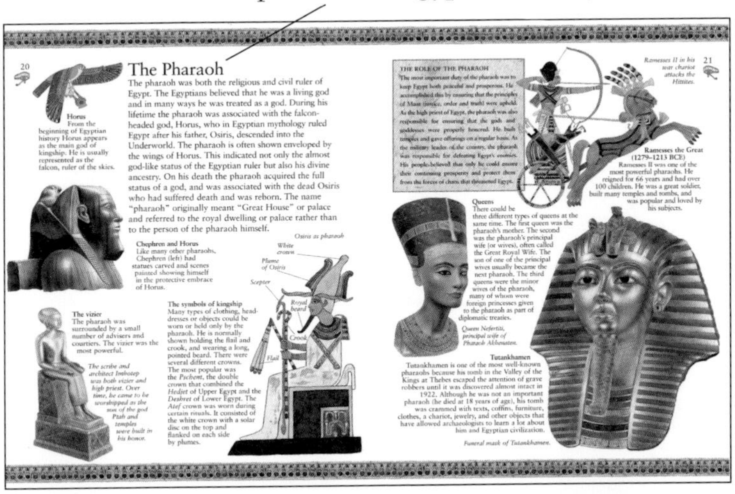

20

The Pharaoh

The pharaoh was both the religious and civil ruler of Egypt. The Egyptians believed that he was a living god and in many ways he was treated as a god. During his lifetime the pharaoh was associated with the falcon-headed god, Horus, who in Egyptian mythology ruled Egypt after his father, Osiris, descended into the Underworld. The pharaoh is often shown enveloped by the wings of Horus. This indicated not only the almost god-like status of the Egyptian ruler but also his divine ancestry. On his death the pharaoh acquired the full status of a god, and was associated with the dead Osiris who had suffered death and was reborn. The name "pharaoh" originally meant "Great House" or palace and referred to the royal dwelling or palace rather than to the person of the pharaoh himself.

Horus From the beginning of Egyptian history Horus appears as the main god of kingship. He is usually represented as the falcon, ruler of the skies.

Chephren and Horus Like many other pharaohs, Chephren (left) had statues carved and scenes painted showing himself in the protective embrace of Horus.

The vizier The pharaoh was surrounded by a small number of advisers and courtiers. The vizier was the most powerful.

The scribe and architect Imhotep was both vizier and high priest. Over time, he came to be worshipped as the son of the god Ptah and temples were built in his honor.

The symbols of kingship Many types of clothing, head-dresses or objects could be worn or held only by the pharaoh. He is normally shown holding the flail and crook, and wearing a long, pointed beard. There were several different crowns. The most popular was the *Pschent*, the double crown that combined the *Hedjet* of Upper Egypt and the *Deshret* of Lower Egypt. The *Atef* crown was worn during certain rituals. It consisted of the white crown with a solar disc on the top and flanked on each side by plumes.

Osiris as pharaoh

THE ROLE OF THE PHARAOH

The most important duty of the pharaoh was to keep Egypt both peaceful and prosperous. He accomplished this by ensuring that the principles of Maat (justice, order and truth) were upheld. As the high priest of Egypt, the pharaoh was also responsible for ensuring that the gods and goddesses were properly honored. He built temples and gave offerings on a regular basis. As the military leader of the country, the pharaoh was responsible for defeating Egypt's enemies. His people believed that only he could ensure their continuing prosperity and protect them from the forces of chaos that threatened Egypt.

Ramesses II in his war chariot attacks the Hittites.

21

Ramesses the Great (1279–1213 BCE) Ramesses II was one of the most powerful pharaohs. He reigned for 66 years and had over 100 children. He was a great soldier, built many temples and tombs, and was popular and loved by his subjects.

Queens There could be three different types of queens at the same time. The first queen was the pharaoh's mother. The second was the pharaoh's principal wife (or wives), often called the Great Royal Wife. The son of one of the principal wives usually became the next pharaoh. The third queens were the minor wives of the pharaoh, many of whom were foreign princesses given to the pharaoh as part of diplomatic treaties.

Queen Nefertiti, principal wife of Pharaoh Akhenaten.

Tutankhamen Tutankhamen is one of the most well-known pharaohs because his tomb in the Valley of the Kings at Thebes escaped the attention of grave robbers until it was discovered almost intact in 1922. Although he was not an important pharaoh (he died at 18 years of age), his tomb was crammed with texts, coffins, furniture, clothes, a chariot, jewelry, and other objects that have allowed archaeologists to learn a lot about him and Egyptian civilization.

Funeral mask of Tutankhamen.

THE CREATION

In the beginning the black waters of Nun enveloped everything and there was darkness and silence everywhere. Then suddenly, out of the watery depths, the pointed tips of a closed lotus flower and a primeval mound appeared. Slowly, they both rose above the water until they were fully formed. The lotus flower then began to uncurl its tightly closed petals and a brilliant yellow light shone from it. When fully open it revealed the small, but perfectly formed figure of the creator, Amun-Ra, sitting in the blaze of light, surrounded by a wonderful perfume. He then turned into a beautiful phoenix bird and flew to the newly formed mound that was shaped like a pyramid. He settled down there stretching out his brightly colored red and gold wings and gave a great cry that echoed in the silence around him.

Amun-Ra became lonely in his watery solitude and so, out of himself, he created a son, Shu, the god of air, and a daughter, the lioness-headed Tefnut, goddess of the dew and of moisture. Amun-Ra was so proud of his children that he wept with happiness.

Shu and Tefnut then conceived a son, Geb, the earth god, and a daughter, Nut, the goddess of the sky. Geb and Nut cared deeply for each other and out of their love came four children. The first was a kind and honorable son, Osiris, who was followed by his brother, Seth. Lastly Nut gave birth to two daughters, the brave and magical Isis, and her gentle and caring sister, Nephthys. These children, unlike their ancestors, lived on earth. After them many more gods and goddesses were born.

Lastly, Amun-Ra ordered the ram-headed god, Khnum, to turn his potter's wheel and fashion man out of clay. Gently breathing life into man, Amun-Ra now realized that he required a place to live, and so he created Egypt. Just as Amun-Ra had emerged from the waters of Nun, so he created the River Nile so that Egypt and its peoples could grow and prosper.

Geography and History

Ancient Egyptian civilization is one of the oldest in the world. It grew up in the fertile lands along the River Nile over 5,000 years ago. Egypt is sometimes called "the gift of the Nile," because the river's annual flood deposits rich black soil on the flat land. In prehistoric times, as the waters withdrew, farmers learned to plant their crops in the muddy flats. Most years the harvests were good and the civilization along the river's banks thrived and grew into one of the most splendid the world has ever known. The Egyptians called the fruitful river valley *kemet*, "the black land," and they referred to themselves as *remet-en-kemet*, "the people of the black land." The Nile is flanked by deserts and the Egyptians called these barren lands *deshret*, "the red land."

This painting from a mummy case shows Amun-Ra's son Shu as he lifts his daughter Nut, the sky goddess, away from Geb, the prince of the earth.

Egyptian prehistory

The time from about 5500 BCE to 3100 BCE is known as the Predynastic period. At that time Egypt was divided into the "Two Lands" of Upper and Lower Egypt. Upper Egypt consisted of the narrow Nile Valley as far north as Memphis, where the river fanned out into the Delta region of Lower Egypt. Each land had its own culture. However, the people of Lower Egypt gradually adopted the customs of Upper Egypt and the two cultures merged.

Unification of the Two Lands

A pharaoh called Narmer (or Menes) is believed to have unified Upper and Lower Egypt around 3100 BCE. A piece of carved green slate, called the Narmer Palette *(right)*, is the first record we have of a king wearing both the *Hedjet*, the white crown of Upper Egypt and the *Deshret*, the red crown of Lower Egypt. Menes made his capital at Memphis, strategically positioned just south of the Delta, from where he could rule both lands.

Back of the Narmer Palette (below) showing the king wearing the white crown.

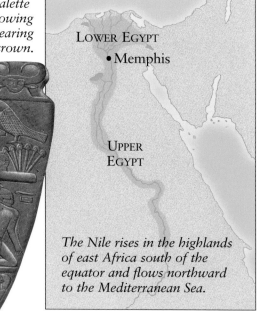

LOWER EGYPT

• Memphis

UPPER EGYPT

The Nile rises in the highlands of east Africa south of the equator and flows northward to the Mediterranean Sea.

Although Egyptian civilization was based on the Nile, the ancient Egyptians did not think of the river as a god. Hapy, often represented as a bull with a sun disc between its horns, was the god of the flood.

The Nile (left) is shown as a plump blue man. He is holding a palm-rib that was the hieroglyph (letter) for year. He also has a small palm-rib tucked into his headband.

The Egyptian calendar

The Egyptians based their calendar on the annual cycle of the Nile. A year had 360 days, plus five extra at the end. The year was divided into three seasons: *akhet*, time of flood; *peret*, time of sowing; and *shemu*, time of harvest. The New Year began in mid-July when the flood began. Each season lasted four months. Months were divided into three weeks of ten days each.

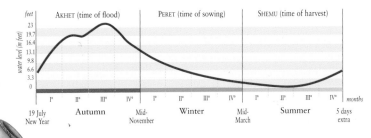

This man, known as "Ginger" from the color of his hair, was buried in Predynastic times.

The head of this ceremonial mace (a weapon used in close combat) shows a ruler of Predynastic Egypt. Because he is wearing the crown of Upper Egypt and is shown with a scorpion, archaeologists called him King Scorpion.

Predynastic burials and grave goods

During this early period the Egyptians buried their dead in a curled-up position directly into the burning desert sands. The heat of the sand drew the body's moisture from it, so preventing decay. At this time only a few simple grave goods were placed in the tomb. These included pottery, palettes, beads, ivory combs, and figurines. Examining these tombs has helped archaeologists understand more about the material culture of Predynastic Egypt.

The flood

The amount of the yearly flood was very important. Too much water meant the destruction of villages, while too little water led to drought and famine. At various points along the Nile the Egyptians set up Nilometers. These were steps from which the water level could be measured. From these they could tell if it would be a good or a bad year for farming.

OSIRIS AND SETH

As the Pharaoh of Egypt, Osiris ruled his country with wisdom and kindness. Osiris hated violence and he chose to civilize the Egyptians in a gentle manner. He showed them how to grow crops so that they could feed themselves. He taught them the law so that they learned good and just behavior. Finally, he instructed them on how to worship the gods to ensure that Egypt prospered.

Things went well in Egypt until Seth, Osiris's wicked brother, who was deeply jealous of him, schemed to oust Osiris from the Egyptian throne. Seth held a lavish banquet and invited Osiris and all the gods and goddesses. During the evening Seth presented a magnificent wooden and gold chest to his guests and invited them to lie inside, promising that he would give it to the one who fitted it best. But Seth had slyly built the chest to fit only Osiris's exact measurements. When Osiris was persuaded to climb into the chest, Seth quickly slammed down the lid, sealed it, and threw it into the Nile where it soon drifted out to sea. The beautiful gilded chest became Osiris's coffin.

When Isis heard what had happened she searched far and wide for her beloved husband. After many months, she found his coffin in the palace at Byblos. Returning home with her gentle Osiris, Isis hid the coffin in the marshes in Lower Egypt. But one night, while she lay sleeping, Seth discovered the coffin. When he saw Osiris's body inside he became red with anger. In a violent rage he tore the body into fourteen pieces and scattered them throughout Egypt. Seth now believed that, at last, he was the only contender for the throne.

Then Isis learned of Seth's savage behavior and, with the patience of great love, she began another long search, this time to gather the pieces of Osiris's body. Each time she found a piece, she built a shrine to honor her dead husband, tricking Seth into believing that she was burying his body. When Isis had collected all the pieces together she used her powerful magic to bring Osiris back to life for just one night. During the night they conceived their son Horus.

Now that Egypt had a legitimate heir to the throne, Osiris descended to the Underworld to rule as the King of the Dead. He showed the Egyptian people that, like him, they would have eternal life, and that their spirits, like his own, would live again after death.

Egyptian Religion

The Egyptians believed that there was a constant battle in the world between the forces of chaos and the forces of order. For life to continue, and for the sun to rise every day, a balance had to be struck between these two forces. As the son of the sun god, the pharaoh was of central importance in maintaining this balance. Because the pharaoh could not be everywhere at once, he delegated some of his duties to priests. The priesthood became very powerful.

Priests are usually shown wearing a leopard skin.

Image of the Ba, from the Book of the Dead.

The Ka and the Ba
The Egyptians believed that a person consisted not only of a body, but also had two spiritual forms, called the Ka and the Ba. The Ba was a bird with a human head that left the body during the day but returned to the tomb at night to live in the mummy. The Ka represented the dead person's spirit and was thought to live in the tomb. An Egyptian funerary text described how *"a thousand loaves of bread and jars of beer"* were required *"for the Ka of the deceased."*

Temples
Egyptian temples were not like Christian churches where people go to worship their god. Only a few people, normally priests, could enter the main doors of the temple. Even fewer could pass through the series of courtyards and doors leading to the cult statue of the god or goddess to whom the temple was dedicated.

Priests
The pharaoh was the high priest. In theory, only he could enter the holy of holies in each temple and carry out the service required by the god. In practice, the pharaoh delegated this job to priests who washed, clothed and gave offerings to the cult statue of the gods on a daily basis. Priests had a strict code of conduct. They had to be very clean, wear sandals made of papyrus and clothes made of linen. They could not wear wool or leather clothes.

Feast days
Each temple had many religious and feast days when the image of the god was carried in procession, usually in a ceremonial boat, from one temple to another.

SANCTUARY Where the shrine with a statue of the god or goddess was kept.

Roofed, columned hall.

Front Courtyard, open to the sky.

The afterlife

The Egyptians believed in life after death. To have an afterlife though, people had to be devoted to the gods and behave well while they lived. They also had to make special preparations when they died. These included mummifying (preserving) the body and preparing the tomb (for example, by putting food and grave goods near the body).

For the deceased to survive in the afterlife the relatives, usually the eldest son, had to bring food to the tomb every day. This was often a costly burden on the family.

Model of servants from a tomb.

GODS AND GODDESSES

The ancient Egyptians believed in so many different gods that it is hard to keep track of them all! Egypt was divided into 42 districts (called "nomes") and each one had its own local gods. However, some gods, such as Osiris, Horus, Hathor, Isis, Anubis, Thoth, and Bes, were worshipped throughout Egypt. They each had their own symbols and could also be represented by special animals. The goddess Hathor, for example, was often shown with a woman's face and cow's ears. Sometimes she was represented simply by a cow wearing a headdress of a sun disc flanked by two horns. Most Egyptian gods and goddesses were associated with a particular town where they were worshipped. Denderah became the center of the goddess Hathor, where priests attended to her temple rituals and worshippers could bring offerings.

Tomb models

Models of tools and food were placed in tombs for the dead person to use in the afterlife. Rich people also placed models of *shabtis* (farm laborers) in their tombs to do all the hard agricultural work (plowing, irrigating, cultivating and harvesting) that they thought would need doing in the afterlife just as it did on earth.

Mummies

The Egyptians mummified their dead because they believed that the body had to stay in a recognizable form for the "Ka," the dead person's spirit, to live in. If the body decayed, the person would not have an afterlife. The brain and internal organs were removed through small cuts. The body was then placed in special salt crystals for 40 days to dry out before being washed, bandaged in fine, scented linen and placed in the coffin.

Procession with the god Khnum being carried in a boat.

Many coffins were richly decorated.

AMUN-RA'S NIGHTLY JOURNEY

Every day the creator and sun god, Amun-Ra, spent twelve hours journeying across the sky in his solar boat. At night, taking the form of the ram-headed god, he descended into the dark, hot, windless depths of the Underworld in order to defeat the forces of chaos that were always threatening Egypt's stability. Every night his solar boat was towed through twelve different regions and in each one a demon waited to challenge his authority.

As the sun god approached each region his light blazed forth, awakening his enemies from their silent sleep. Cobras that spat fire and snakes with wings and many heads were aroused during the twelve hours that it took Amun-Ra to travel across this deadly western realm to rise again, once more, in the east. The fiercest of all the monsters that attempted to destroy Amun- Ra was the snake Apophis. This wicked creature had no soul and was condemned to a life of chaos and evil. As the solar boat approached Apophis, goddesses leapt forward and slashed the snake with knives, leaving Apophis slithering and writhing in pain on the ground, as the boat passed him by. All the evil-doers, who were the enemies of Amun-Ra, were destroyed. They were shown no mercy; bound and decapitated they were thrown into pits of fire where their souls were burned.

At the twelfth hour Amun-Ra reached his eastern destination. Taking the form of Khephri, the scarab beetle who emerged daily out of his ball of dung, he was reborn as the sun, signalling the safe arrival of a new day. Amun-Ra underwent this perilous journey through the Underworld every night. By completing the journey he showed he had triumphed over the dark forces that constantly threatened Egypt's very existence.

Canopic jars
The brain and other internal organs were preserved separately from the body. Once removed, they were dried in salts then placed in special little jars called canopic jars. These were placed alongside the coffin in the tomb.

The Weighing of the Heart ceremony
The Egyptians believed that the heart was the center or "brain" of an individual. One of the tests dead people had to take to pass through the Underworld consisted in weighing the heart on scales against Maat, the goddess of justice and truth, who was symbolized by a feather. Thoth, the god of wisdom, stood close by to record the result. If the heart and the feather did not balance equally, the heart would be eaten and the deceased would have no afterlife.

Burial Customs

The Egyptians had very elaborate burial customs. Between about 2700 BCE and 1650 BCE they built hundreds of huge pyramids as monumental tombs for their dead pharaohs. The pyramids, regarded as one of the Seven Wonders of the Ancient World, are the only Wonder that still survives. The Egyptians had many other customs and rituals to prepare the dead person's body and spirit for the afterlife.

A tomb painting of Anubis, the jackal-headed god and protector of the dead, embalming and preparing a dead man for the tomb.

Cheops's boat
Models of boats were often placed in tombs to help the dead on their journeys through the Underworld. A dismantled boat belonging to Cheops was found buried next to his pyramid. It measured 141 feet (43 m) and was made out of precious cedar wood.

The Opening of the Mouth ceremony
This was an important funeral ritual. During the ceremony a priest would touch the mouth of the mummy with an adze to restore its senses. Life was thought to return to the body so that it could speak, see and hear.

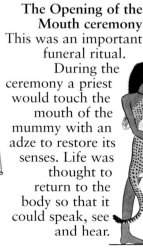

The step pyramid of Pharaoh Djoser at Saqqara.

The most famous, and the largest, of all the pyramids is at Giza. It belonged to the Pharaoh Cheops (about 2590–2568 BCE). The pyramid, which was originally 479 feet (146 m) high, was built of granite. The Great Pyramid also had an outer casing of fine limestone that came from the quarries at Tura.

The pyramids at Giza are guarded by a huge stone statue called the Sphinx.

The meaning of the pyramids

There are many theories about the pyramids. According to one they represent the primeval mound of creation and were home to Ra, the sun god. Another claims that the golden peak crowning each pyramid represented the sun's rays and that the pyramids acted as huge staircases for the pharaoh to ascend to heaven.

Development of the pyramids

There were two stages to the development of the pyramids. True pyramids grew out of step pyramids, which had developed from the earlier mud-brick mastaba tombs. The earliest and most famous step pyramid is at Saqqara. It was built by the architect Imhotep for Pharaoh Djoser during the 3rd Dynasty in about 2650 BCE. The first smooth-sided pyramid was built at Dashur in the reign of Pharaoh Snefru in the 4th Dynasty. We do not know exactly how pyramids were built, but archaeologists think that a series of ramps and levers were used to haul the stones into place.

A pyramid was usually the focal point of a burial complex. It was surrounded by secondary pyramids and mastaba tombs, probably for the king's wives, relatives and courtiers.

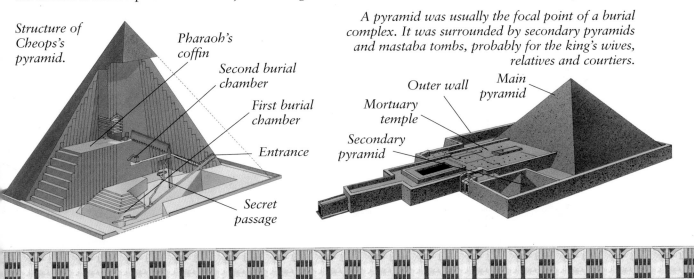

Structure of Cheops's pyramid.

Pharaoh's coffin

Second burial chamber

First burial chamber

Entrance

Secret passage

Outer wall

Main pyramid

Mortuary temple

Secondary pyramid

THE BATTLE FOR KINGSHIP

When Horus grew up he decided to challenge his wicked and cunning uncle Seth for the throne. Horus believed that, as the son of Osiris, he was the rightful ruler of Egypt. So he appealed to the gods, demanding that they make him pharaoh. But Seth was outraged, maintaining that as the strongest of all the gods he should be king.

After much discussion the gods decided to award Horus the throne. But Seth would not accept defeat and challenged Horus to a contest. Each god had to turn himself into a hippopotamus and remain submerged under the waters of the Nile. If either emerged within three months, he would lose the throne. But Isis, Horus's mother, feared for her son's safety. She was afraid that Seth would try to kill Horus under the water.

Isis threw a copper harpoon into the Nile, hoping to hit Seth. But it was Horus that leapt up. "Mother," he cried in pain, "you have hit me, your son!" Isis quickly withdrew her harpoon. Aiming once again she thrust it back into the Nile. This time she hit Seth. "Dearest sister," Seth cried cunningly, "do not hurt me, your brother." At this, Isis once again withdrew her harpoon.

As Isis had ruined the first contest Seth challenged Horus again. This time they were to race down the Nile in boats of stone. Now it was Horus's turn to be cunning. He knew that stone could not float. So he built a wooden boat and covered it with limestone to make it look like stone. Seth foolishly made his boat out of a mountain peak, which sank as soon as it hit the water. Seth was furious. How dare Horus trick him! Angrily Seth transformed himself into a hippopotamus and attacked Horus's boat.

Desperate to end the fighting between Horus and Seth, the gods finally turned to Osiris for advice. Osiris insisted that his son Horus was the rightful king and threatened to order savages from the Underworld to eat the gods' hearts if they did not respect his wishes. Fearing Osiris's wrath the gods immediately crowned Horus as the pharaoh of all Egypt.

Horus
From the beginning of Egyptian history Horus appears as the main god of kingship. He is usually represented as the falcon, ruler of the skies.

The Pharaoh

The pharaoh was both the religious and civil ruler of Egypt. The Egyptians believed that he was a living god and in many ways he was treated as a god. During his lifetime the pharaoh was associated with the falcon-headed god, Horus, who in Egyptian mythology ruled Egypt after his father, Osiris, descended into the Underworld. The pharaoh is often shown enveloped by the wings of Horus. This indicated not only the almost god-like status of the Egyptian ruler but also his divine ancestry. On his death the pharaoh acquired the full status of a god, and was associated with the dead Osiris who had suffered death and was reborn. The name "pharaoh" originally meant "Great House" or palace and referred to the royal dwelling or palace rather than to the person of the pharaoh himself.

Chephren and Horus
Like many other pharaohs, Chephren (left) had statues carved and scenes painted showing himself in the protective embrace of Horus.

Osiris as pharaoh

White crown

Plume of Osiris

Scepter

Royal beard

Crook

Flail

The vizier
The pharaoh was surrounded by a small number of advisers and courtiers. The vizier was the most powerful.

The scribe and architect Imhotep was both vizier and high priest. Over time, he came to be worshipped as the son of the god Ptah and temples were built in his honor.

The symbols of kingship
Many types of clothing, head-dresses or objects could be worn or held only by the pharaoh. He is normally shown holding the flail and crook, and wearing a long, pointed beard. There were several different crowns. The most popular was the *Pschent*, the double crown that combined the *Hedjet* of Upper Egypt and the *Deshret* of Lower Egypt. The *Atef* crown was worn during certain rituals. It consisted of the white crown with a solar disc on the top and flanked on each side by plumes.

THE ROLE OF THE PHARAOH

The most important duty of the pharaoh was to keep Egypt both peaceful and prosperous. He accomplished this by ensuring that the principles of Maat (justice, order and truth) were upheld. As the high priest of Egypt, the pharaoh was also responsible for ensuring that the gods and goddesses were properly honored. He built temples and gave offerings on a regular basis. As the military leader of the country, the pharaoh was responsible for defeating Egypt's enemies. His people believed that only he could ensure their continuing prosperity and protect them from the forces of chaos that threatened Egypt.

Ramesses II in his war chariot attacks the Hittites.

Ramesses the Great (1279–1213 BCE)

Ramesses II was one of the most powerful pharaohs. He reigned for 66 years and had over 100 children. He was a great soldier, built many temples and tombs, and was popular and loved by his subjects.

Queens

There could be three different types of queens at the same time. The first queen was the pharaoh's mother. The second was the pharaoh's principal wife (or wives), often called the Great Royal Wife. The son of one of the principal wives usually became the next pharaoh. The third queens were the minor wives of the pharaoh, many of whom were foreign princesses given to the pharaoh as part of diplomatic treaties.

Queen Nefertiti, principal wife of Pharaoh Akhenaten.

Tutankhamen

Tutankhamen is one of the most well-known pharaohs because his tomb in the Valley of the Kings at Thebes escaped the attention of grave robbers until it was discovered almost intact in 1922. Although he was not an important pharaoh (he died at 18 years of age), his tomb was crammed with texts, coffins, furniture, clothes, a chariot, jewelry, and other objects that have allowed archaeologists to learn a lot about him and Egyptian civilization.

Funeral mask of Tutankhamen.

THOTH BRINGS HATHOR BACK

One day the beautiful goddess Hathor quarrelled with her father, the sun god Ra. She was so angry she turned herself into a lioness and left Egypt for Nubia where she roamed the countryside destroying and killing anything that dared to cross her path. When Ra learned that his daughter had left he was deeply saddened; Hathor, the eye of the sun, no longer shone brightly in Egypt. So Ra asked his wisest and most learned scribe, the god Thoth, to go to Nubia and bring his lovely daughter home. On hearing Ra's request Thoth, knowing Hathor's wrath, feared for his life. After consulting his own writings and his book of magic, he decided to approach the goddess, not as himself, but as a lowly and meek baboon.

Thoth traveled south to Nubia and found the goddess. He tried to entice her back to Egypt with delicious fruits, delicacies and sweet memories of her home and her father. On hearing these the goddess began to weep for all that she had lost. Thoth invited her to accompany him back to Egypt and offered his protection during their journey. But the goddess laughed and ridiculed the little baboon, saying that he was no match for the power and strength of a lion. At this

Thoth smiled and began to tell her the tale of the lion and the mouse. Although reluctant to follow Thoth, Hathor wanted to hear his tale, and so, slowly, the two of them made their way homeward.

"A fierce lion was raging through the forest," Thoth began, "trying to find a man to punish for all the cruelties he had inflicted upon the creatures of the forest. Hearing a shrill squeal beneath his large paw, he looked down to find that he was about to tread on a tiny mouse. The mouse begged the lion not to hurt him and promised that one day he might be of service. The lion roared with laughter at such a preposterous idea, but he let the mouse go free before going on his way. Soon afterward the lion fell into a deep pit. A man came and bound his legs with leather straps and left him there to die. Suddenly, the little mouse appeared and, gnawing through the straps, set the lion free. The lion was shamefaced in front of his new friend. He gathered him up in his mane, and the two set off toward the mountains." "Thus," concluded Thoth, "the smaller and weaker of the two helped the stronger." Hathor smiled gently, as they continued on their journey back to Egypt.

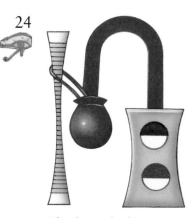

This hieroglyphic sign shows the equipment a scribe used to write. The palette on the right contains red and black cakes of paint. Above there is a waterbag and, to the left, a reed brush or papyrus smoother. The scribe made ink by mixing the paints with a little water.

The Scribe

Very few children went to school in ancient Egypt and most people could not read or write. A tiny percentage of boys from good families went to special schools where they learned to be scribes. Being a scribe was an important job and could lead to a position of power. The boys, who started school at about the age of five, learned reading, writing and arithmetic. They studied hieratic writing first and then hieroglyphics, which were much more complicated. They had to write out long sentences to practice their skills. When fully trained, their work ranged from writing letters for those who could not write, teaching other scribes and calculating taxes on the large estates. There are many pictures of scribes assessing quantities of grain or counting cows and flocks of geese.

Painted limestone statue of a scribe in the traditional cross-legged position in which they worked.

Egyptian scripts

There were three main scripts: hieroglyphic, hieratic and demotic. The hieroglyphic script had about 750 picture and sound signs (hieroglyphs). It was used and understood by only a few people. Hieratic was a form of everyday writing based on, and used at the same time as, hieroglyphs. It was written from right to left and its symbols could be written far more quickly than hieroglyphs. Hieratic was used for informal correspondence such as letters, literature and documents. Demotic was used from the 7th century BCE and, like hieratic, was a speedy, everyday script.

Thoth, god of the scribe, was often shown as a baboon.

Papyrus

The Egyptians were the first to make paper. They were famous in the ancient world for the quality of their papyrus. The long-stemmed papyrus plant grew particularly well in the marshes of the Delta. It was used not only for making paper but also for ropes, baskets and in shipbuilding.

Scribe at work, surrounded by his tools.

Scribes' tools

Many statues of scribes show them with their tools—a palette and a roll of papyrus. Scribes' palettes were light and easy to carry around. Because papyrus was expensive, scribes practiced on or used wooden boards, leather sheets or ostraca (bits of broken stone or pottery) for their work.

Palette

Tools used for preparing the papyrus.

Deciphering hieroglyphics

For a long time no one could read the writings left by the ancient Egyptians. The break-through came in 1822 when a Frenchman, Jean-François Champollion, studied and compared the three texts— in hieroglyphic, demotic and Greek—inscribed on the Rosetta Stone *(right)*.

Egyptian girls did not go to school. They stayed at home and learned from their mothers how to cook and weave. However, it seems that some women did learn to read and write. At the village of Deir el-Medina, women appear to have both sent and received letters.

FUNERARY TEXTS

The earliest funerary texts, called the Pyramid Texts, were inscribed on the walls of pyramids dating from the Old Kingdom and First Intermediate Period (about 2780 to 2050 BCE). They consisted of about 800 spells designed to guarantee a safe journey into the afterlife. By the Middle Kingdom (2050 to about 1600 BCE), the Pyramid Texts had been replaced by the Coffin Texts. These texts had about 1,000 spells, many based on the earlier Pyramid Texts. At first only pharaohs had used these texts, but by the Middle Kingdom many ordinary people were also using them. The Book of the Dead was introduced around 1600 BCE at the beginning of the period known as the New Kingdom. It had about 200 spells. Although these spells could be written on amulets, they were mostly written on papyrus and then placed inside the coffin or within statues of Osiris.

THE BOATING PARTY

Pharaoh Snefru was bored and restless. He was wandering aimlessly around his palace when he met his chief priest, Djada-em-ankh. Seeing the pharaoh's bored expression, the priest suggested that an outing on the lakes would refresh his spirit. "But choose only beautiful young maidens to row," the chief priest suggested, "for their beauty will combine with the loveliness of Egypt's green fields and shores, to lift your spirits."

Snefru agreed, and twenty of Egypt's most beautiful young women, with their hair newly braided and dressed in clothes of finely meshed fishnets, were selected to row Snefru across the waters using oars of ebony, gold and sandalwood.

Out on the lake, Snefru lay back in the boat, enjoying the gentle sweep of the oars in the water, the sweet perfume of the lotus flowers on the lake, and the beauty of the women rowing in unison. Suddenly, he heard a splash and then the women stopped rowing. When he asked what was wrong, one of the maidens, the chief rower, cried out that her beautiful new turquoise pendant had fallen into the water. The pharaoh, seeing how distraught she was, told her not to worry and to keep on rowing because he would give her a new pendant. When she refused, Snefru was furious. He summoned Djada-em-ankh and insisted that the chief priest use his magical powers to restore calm to the boating party. So

Djada-em-ankh divided the waters in two like a blanket and folded one half back upon the other. Looking down at the bottom of the lake, Djada-em-ankh spotted the turquoise pendant lying on top of an old broken piece of pottery. Quickly retrieving it, he returned the pendant to its owner and, uttering another magic spell, restored the lake to its original calm. Snefru was so delighted by these events that he invited everyone to a magnificent feast at the palace that evening.

Some women
worked as
musicians and
dancers. The girl
in the center is
enjoying herself
as she dances.
Women may also
have worked as
professional
mourners.

Tomb paintings
show women
from poorer
families doing
farm work. This
woman is
sowing seeds
from a basket
into the freshly
plowed earth.

Harp   Lute   Flutes   Lyre

Women and Family Life

Egyptian women led freer lives and had more
rights than most other women in the ancient
world. Legally, they could inherit, own and
manage their own property. They could make
loans, rent land and run their own businesses.
Egyptian women did not need an escort to
accompany them when they went out, they did
not have to cover their heads in public, and they
were not restricted to certain areas in the home.
Despite these freedoms, women are not recorded
in positions of power. Most women married
young and devoted themselves to their families.

*Many statues and
paintings show women in
tight-fitting dresses like this
servant woman (right).
However, since most
clothes were made of linen,
it seems more likely that
they wore loose-
fitting clothes
like those the
entertainers and
mourners (left)
are wearing.*

Portrait of a royal family. Pharaoh Akhenaten (1350–1334 BCE) and Queen Nefertiti are shown with three of their six daughters on their knees.

Although marriages were frequently arranged, many couples seem to have been happy. There are love poems and statues showing husbands and wives of equal height sitting closely together.

The Family

The family played a central role in Egyptian society. Families normally consisted of a man, his wife and their children.

Marriage

The main purpose of marriage was to have children. There was no marriage ceremony. Instead a marriage contract would be drawn up in which the husband generally pledged to protect his wife. The wife, in turn, promised to bring a dowry. After this the wife moved into her husband's house. With the exception of the pharaoh, Egyptian men usually only had one wife. Couples could divorce, and it was quite usual for widowed or divorced people to remarry.

Egyptian goddesses

Isis and Hathor were the two most important and popular goddesses throughout Egyptian history. As the wife of Osiris and the mother of Horus, Isis was seen as a mother goddess and a protector of children. Hathor was regarded as a goddess of beauty and love and the protector of women during childbirth. Both goddesses were very popular with women and there were many temples dedicated to them.

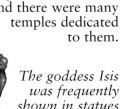

The goddess Isis was frequently shown in statues holding her son Horus.

Jewelry and cosmetics

Egyptian women and men both wore jewelry and used cosmetics. They stored them in beautifully decorated boxes and exquisitely shaped vases and bottles.

OCCUPATIONS

Most Egyptian women worked in the home doing household chores and caring for children. They also helped in the fields at busy times, such as harvest. Although few Egyptian women were employed in government or held political power, some other occupations were open to them. Poor women could find work as servants in wealthy households. Women could also be musicians or priestesses in the temples or they could become dancers, professional mourners, musicians and midwives. They also worked in some industries, such as cloth-making.

THE MAGICIAN

ne day Pharaoh Khufu was bored and so he invited his son, Prince Hardedef, to tell him a magical story. Instead, the Prince told his father of a real magician called Djedi. "He is 110 years old and lives in a town called Djed-Snefru," Hardedef told his father. "He is, moreover, famed not only for his huge appetite, for he eats 500 loaves of bread and half an ox a day, but also for his ability to tame wild lions and to join the severed heads of wild creatures. It is also said that he knows how many secret rooms there are in the chamber of Thoth." At this Khufu became excited and commanded Hardedef to bring Djedi to the royal court, for the

pharaoh wanted to copy the secrets of Thoth's sanctuary into his own tomb.

At his father's request, Hardedef brought Djedi to the palace to meet him. The pharaoh inquired whether it was true that Djedi could reunite the heads and bodies of decapitated animals. When Djedi said that it was true, a goose was brought to the court and killed. Its head and body were then placed at opposite ends of the room. Djedi uttered his magic spells and the goose's body and head suddenly began to move toward each other. Before a spellbound audience, its body joined its head and the goose, now alive, cackled noisily. Then an ox and a long-legged bird were brought into the court and the experiment was repeated. Once again, both creatures were brought back to life when Djedi performed his magic.

Fascinated, Khufu now asked the question that really interested him. "Tell me, how many secret chambers are there in the Sanctuary of Thoth?" Djedi replied that the answer could only be given by the eldest child of Ruddedet— the wife of a powerful priest—who would, one day, rule Egypt.

On hearing this prophecy Khufu grew sad, fearing that his family would lose the Egyptian throne. But when Djedi told Khufu that his own son and grandson would rule Egypt before Ruddedet's children, Khufu smiled again. Knowing the magician's passion for food the pharaoh then rewarded Djedi with 1,000 loaves of bread, an ox, a mountain of vegetables and 100 jugs of beer.

Food and Daily Life

Considering the long span of time that separates us from the ancient Egyptians, archaeologists have been able to learn a surprising amount about how they lived by studying tomb paintings, grave goods (objects found in tombs), works of art and artifacts of all kinds. Literary texts and administrative records also provide precious information.

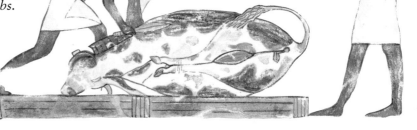

Man cooking beef.

Food

Bread and beer were two main items in the Egyptian diet. But the rich, fertile land also ensured that a variety of fruits and vegetables were grown, including grapes, melons, figs, dates, pomegranates, cucumbers, lettuce, onions, and garlic. There was no sugar in Egypt so they used dates and honey to sweeten their food. Meat and poultry were a luxury that only the rich could afford.

A menu fit for a queen

Archaeologists uncovered a feast at the tomb of the wife of a 2nd Dynasty king. The menu included: ground barley soup, quails, kidney, boiled fish, pigeon stew, beef ribs, bread, round cakes, fruit, cheese, wine, and beer.

Paintings and models of butchers at work have been found in many tombs.

Daily bread

Bread was a staple food for both the rich and the poor. Basic bread was made with flour, yeast, salt, and water, but more elaborate breads were also prepared using spices, milk, butter, and eggs. Until the New Kingdom (about 1600 BCE), bread was made at home by housewives or servants. After that most villages had bakeries.

The painting below shows servants plucking and gutting geese ready for cooking.

Furniture

The average home did not have much furniture. Most pieces were simple and made from wood, although the rich often had furniture inlaid with ebony, gold, and ivory. They slept on beds with mattresses made from rushes. For pillows they used wooden headrests. Chests were used to store clothes and bed linen. Chairs were considered a luxury and the majority of Egyptians had stools to sit on. Small wooden tables were used at mealtimes.

Headrest

Blanket

Bed

Some of the finer walled houses had an enclosed garden with a fish pond and shady trees.

Slippers

Stool

Houses

Houses were built of unbaked mud bricks made of Nile mud that was mixed with straw, placed in molds and left to dry. Unfortunately, as the mud brick crumbled in the strong sun, houses had to be rebuilt frequently. Wealthy people lived in large villas. These had luxuries such as bathrooms and were set in lovely gardens. In contrast, some poorer people lived in houses with only two small rooms. Houses were often more than one storey high and had staircases to the roof. Walls might be painted with bright pictures of the gods, animals or flowers.

Ornamental perfume container

Reconstruction of a worker's house at Deir el-Medina (1567–1085 BCE). The village housed the craftspeople and artists who decorated the royal tombs at Luxor.

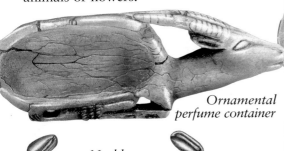

Necklaces

Comb

Storage room for grain

Sleeping quarters   *Living area*   *Cellar*

THE SHIPWRECKED SAILOR'S TALE

My story begins with a trading expedition that I led to the royal mines of the Red Sea. My large ship had a crew of 120 of Egypt's most experienced sailors. Yet we never arrived at our destination. For suddenly a violent storm arose and colossal waves smashed the mast. The boat capsized and I was thrown overboard.

I awoke to find myself marooned, alone, on an island. I was so frightened that I hid among the trees. For three days I ate nothing. Then, desperately hungry, I decided to explore my new home. To my surprise I found wonderful things—figs, grapes, date-palms, cucumbers, fish and birds. I had landed on an enchanted island! Joyously, I lit a fire and gave offerings in thanks to the gods. But suddenly the ground began to move. There was something coming toward me. I froze in terror. As it moved closer I saw that it was a giant golden snake. Rearing up its head the snake demanded, "What are you doing here?" Then to my horror it picked me up in its jaws and carried me to its pit. Gathering my courage I told my tale. Suddenly, the snake became friendly. I would be rescued in four months' time, he told me. "If this is true," I replied, "I shall send you a valuable cargo from Egypt." The snake laughed. "It is I, not you, who is the Prince of Punt!" he said. "My island contains treasures beyond your reckoning. When you leave I will give you such a precious cargo that the pharaoh will richly reward you."

After four months I was rescued and the snake, true to his word, gave me valuable treasures. The pharaoh, delighted with my booty, made me a palace official. The snake's prophecy had been fulfilled. But I have never been able to visit the island again, for it has mysteriously disappeared.

Golden medals in the shape of flies were awarded to soldiers for bravery in battle.

Trade and Expansion

With deserts to the west and to the east, and the Mediterranean Sea to the north, Egypt's natural boundaries kept it safe from foreign invasion for 3,000 years. However, foreign conquest was important to the pharaohs and during the New Kingdom they held an empire that stretched from the River Euphrates in the Middle East to Nubia in Africa. Although it was many centuries before the Egyptians had a system of money, they maintained wide-ranging trade links. Both domestic and foreign trade were conducted by barter (exchange of goods of equal value) or by giving items a value against metal weights and using them for payment.

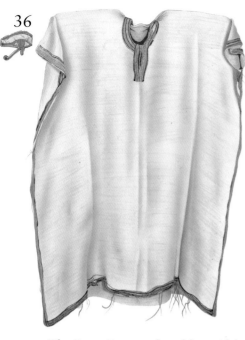

The Egyptians produced beautiful linen cloth and garments for their own use and for export. This heavy linen tunic, with borders and neckline decorated in gold, was found in a tomb.

Tribute and diplomatic gifts

Tribute and diplomatic gifts were two other forms of trade. Royal gifts and payments were exchanged between rulers wishing to cement a good relationship. Sometimes foreign states sent princesses to the pharaohs as gifts. Ramesses II's many foreign wives included two Hittite princesses in addition to princesses from Syria and Babylonia.

A larger empire

During the 12th Dynasty the pharaohs campaigned to increase Egypt's boundaries and many fortresses were built in Nubia to the south. Egypt's frontiers reached their greatest extent in the 18th Dynasty under Thutmose III (1504–1450 BCE). However, it was difficult and costly to maintain such a large territory. Thutmose III, for example, had to fight fourteen battles to quell revolts in Palestine and Syria.

Imports and exports

Gold, papyrus, linen, and grain were Egypt's chief exports and accounted for much of its wealth. The Egyptians imported wood, particularly cedar from Lebanon that was used in ship-building and to make coffins. Ebony and ivory from Africa were used in furniture-making. Incense, myrrh and oils, especially from Punt and Yemen, were used for cosmetics and perfumes and in the mummification process. Copper and iron were imported to make tools and weapons and lapis lazuli came from far-off Afghanistan to be made into jewelry.

Metal weight shaped like a rabbit. Weights like these were used to pay for imports.

Royal cubit for measuring covered in decorated gold leaf.

The back of the Narmer Palette shows the pharaoh wearing the Red Crown of Lower Egypt parading with men holding standards from the various regions of Egypt.

The Battle of Qadesh

One of the most famous battles in Egyptian history took place in 1285 BCE by the city of Qadesh on the River Orontes. It was fought between Ramesses II and the Hittite King Muwatallis for the control of Syria. Ramesses's army numbered 20,000 men, which he divided into four divisions of 5,000. At the Battle of Qadesh both sides suffered heavy losses although Ramesses II claimed it as a victory.

Foreigners and captives

The Egyptians believed that they were superior to all other peoples in the ancient world. Their two main enemies were the Hittites and the Nubians. On many Egyptian temples there are reliefs of bound captives and slaves. These were carved to emphasize Egypt's strength and military prowess to the rest of the world. Mercenaries always formed a large part of the army, but by the time of Amenhophis III captives were also being used and could earn their freedom by serving in the Egyptian army.

Soldiers' training

During the New Kingdom training for Egyptian soldiers was rigorous and took place in special military camps. Recruits had to endure great physical hardships, but although the life of a soldier was very hard, there were many rewards. They could share in the spoils of war and were often given grants of land.

The army

It was not until the New Kingdom that Egypt had an organized professional army made up of infantry and charioteers and led by a commander-in-chief—usually one of the pharaoh's sons.

HOW THE BLESSED LIVED

The Egyptians believed that after they died they would go to an idyllic and prosperous afterlife in the Elysian Fields. These fields would be surrounded by canals and fruit-laden trees and the air would be fragrant with the perfume of flowers and incense. No longer would the Egyptians have to worry about the Nile flooding too much and ruining their crops or flooding too little, causing drought and famine. Instead the canals would irrigate the rich and fertile Egyptian soil and an abundance of barley and emmer wheat would grow. Wine, beer and milk would flow and cakes, oxen and ducks would be eaten. No longer would the Egyptians toil every day in the hot sun behind their ox-drawn plows; instead shabtis, magical servant figures, would labor in the fields.

In the afterlife the Egyptians would spend their time singing, playing games, sailing down the Nile, hunting for birds and fishing in the marshes, feasting, and making offerings to the gods, all among friends and family once more united.

But to reach this prosperous and golden afterlife every Egyptian knew that their spirit had to face a perilous journey when their behavior on earth would be judged. The Judgement of the Soul took place in the Hall of Two Truths where Osiris, seated upon his throne, was surrounded by forty-two judges all carrying sharp knives. On reaching the hall the deceased had first to plead not guilty to crimes such as murder and stealing. Then, showing great courage, the dead person had to address the gods by their individual names and make further statements about their good behavior. "O Bone-Smasher who comes from Hnes; I have not told lies," and "Oh Blood-Eater who comes from Slaughterplace; I have not slain sacred cattle." Finally the deceased's spirit had to give a great shout of "I am pure, I am pure, I am pure."

The next stage of the judgement was even more terrifying. Anubis, the jackal-headed god, weighed the deceased's heart against the feather of truth. If the heart and the feather did not balance, the Devourer, an ugly creature that was part lion, part hippopotamus and part crocodile, stood by eagerly waiting to eat the deceased's heart. If found pure, the deceased would be taken to Osiris and the doors to the Elysian Fields would be opened and they would walk out into the land of the blessed.

Life along the Nile

Life in Egypt centered largely on the Nile. As a result of the annual flood and the rich soil it left behind, Egypt was an agricultural society. For most people daily work involved planting and harvesting crops, animal care and other farming tasks. But the Nile was not only the source of farming, it was also the main transport route for travel and trade. Popular pastimes such as hunting, fishing and sailing also took place on the river.

Painted wooden model of an agricultural worker. The majority of Egyptians worked on the land as farm workers. They produced the surplus of food that allowed the minority of soldiers, scribes, artists, priests, and rulers to prosper.

Livestock

Cattle and oxen were prized possessions. Rich Egyptians often had pictures of themselves done with large herds of cattle. Cattle produced milk and meat and were also used for plowing. All meat was expensive but ox meat was the most highly valued. It was used in temple offerings. Sheep and goats were kept for their milk, meat and wool.

Grain Harvest

Wheat, barley, and flax were the main crops. The Egyptians grew three types of wheat: emmer, einkhorn, and spelt. The ground was prepared using oxen or hoes. Then the seed was scattered by hand and animals trampled it in. Wooden sickles with flint teeth were used to cut the grain and donkeys took it to the threshing floor, where the wheat was separated from the chaff and the grain stored in granaries.

The Egyptians made and drank both red and white wine. The wall painting from a tomb at Thebes (below) shows men picking grapes.

Wine

Egypt had its own vineyards and also imported wine from Syria and Palestine and, later, from Greece. The grapes were pressed and the juice left to ferment in vats or amphorae (earthenware jars). After several years, when the wine had matured, it was flavored using spices, honey or dates. The Egyptians also made wine from figs, pomegranates, and dates.

Fish

Fish were an important source of food. Fishermen used nets and traps to catch them. Although some images of harpooning have been found, it was considered more as a sport. There was a large variety of fish in the Nile and Diodorus, a Greek traveler to Egypt, recorded that twenty-two different types of fish could be found in Fayum lake in northern Egypt. Most fish were eaten fresh, although some were salted to preserve them for later consumption.

Boats

Boats were the main means of transport in Egypt. The Nile was a natural highway and people and goods almost always traveled on the river. During the Old Kingdom the huge quantities of heavy stone used to build the pyramids were hauled the length of Egypt in wooden boats.

Shaduf

In the earliest days the Egyptians used jars to water their land. During the 18th Dynasty the shaduf was invented. Using a bucket and counterweight it transferred water from the Nile into canals, so allowing the irrigation of much larger fields.

During the Middle Kingdom statues of blue faïence hippopotamuses with flowers on their backs were made to symbolize the Nile's fertility.

THE HIPPOPOTAMUS

The hippopotamus is now extinct in Egypt, but in ancient times there were many in the Nile. They were often a menace, capsizing boats in the river and causing damage to fields and crops. Hippopotamus hunts were a popular pastime, particularly for pharaohs. In Egyptian mythology the hippopotamus represented Seth, Osiris's evil brother. Pictures of hippopotamus hunts frequently show how the pharaoh, representing good, overcomes evil by killing them.

Animals in Egyptian Society

Animals played an important role in the lives of the ancient Egyptians. Many were domesticated and used to produce meat, milk and wool, or as beasts of burden to carry heavy loads or to pull plows or carts. Others, such as dogs, cats and monkeys, were kept as pets. Many wild animals, including the snakes and scorpions that came from the desert, and the hippopotamuses and crocodiles that lived in the Nile, were feared. Other Nile animals, such as birds and fish, were an important source of food. What is unique about the Egyptians' relationship to animals is the way they associated so many of them with their gods and goddesses and with magical or supernatural events.

This gold hawk's head, with its piercing eyes and gold crown, dates from Old Kingdom times.

Animals as symbols

Animals were often used to represent beliefs or people. A hawk or a lion could represent the pharaoh. Animals could also be used to represent an area. A crown with a cobra identified Wadjet, goddess of Lower Egypt, while one with a vulture indicated Nekhbet, the goddess of Upper Egypt. The pharaoh, as the ruler of both Upper and Lower Egypt, had both the cobra and the vulture among his symbols.

Animals and literature

Animals were popular in Egyptian literature. In stories, scribes used animals as main characters or to highlight a moral. One papyrus tells of two animals known to be enemies, the lion and the antelope, sitting together to play a friendly game of senet.

SACRED ANIMALS

The Egyptians regarded many animals as sacred to the gods. The cat was sacred to the goddess Bastet, the cow to the goddess Hathor, the crocodile to the god Sobek, and scorpions were associated with the goddess Selket. Late in Egyptian history many animals were mummified and brought by worshippers as offerings to the gods in their temples. In Saqqara at least four million mummified ibises have been found. The Apis bull was believed to be the earthly form of the god Ptah and was thus a living god. When the old bull died an identical successor was chosen.

Many gods were represented by figures with human bodies and animal heads. This wall painting shows the union of the gods Ra and Osiris as a mummy with a ram's head. The horns supporting the sun disc between them are those of a sheep that is now extinct.

Exotic animals

Animals such as panthers, ostriches and giraffes were often given to the pharaoh as tribute. In Alexandria during the 3rd century BCE the Pharaoh Ptolemy II Philadelphus held a famous procession with many exotic creatures. There were also new varieties of Ethiopian and Arabian sheep. By introducing new strains of sheep into Egypt Ptolemy II hoped to increase the variety of wool available for domestic use and for export.

This beautiful painting shows the scribe Nebamun hunting birds among the papyrus plants along the Nile. In his right hand he holds three herons that act as decoys. He is accompanied by his wife and daughter, and also by their pet cat, which is energetically joining in the hunt.

Many animals were used in the Egyptians' hieroglyphic script. The owl stood for the letter "m." The owl sign is very unusual because it shows the bird's head looking toward the observer. Almost all Egyptian drawings of human and animal heads are shown in profile, as in the wall painting (below).

Hunting

The earliest Egyptians lived by hunting the wild animals along the Nile. Even after farming had been introduced people continued to hunt. For the pharaoh and other rich people, hunting was a favorite sport. Lions and deer were hunted in the desert and hippopotamuses, crocodiles, and bulls in the marshes. Elephant hunts were popular, too. There are many tomb paintings of royal hunts that often show the pharaoh as a hunter destroying any danger that threatened the safety of his kingdom. Hunting became a symbol of Egyptian kingship.

GLOSSARY

adze Similar to an axe, a tool for cutting and shaping wood.

annual Occurring once every year.

archaeologist Someone who studies ancient civilizations.

barren Empty, consisting of little sustenance.

ceremony A process or ritual designed to celebrate a special occasion.

chariot A horse-drawn carriage used in ancient warfare and racing.

civilization A group of people with common culture living together for a long period of time.

drought A long period of little or no rain.

dynasty A succession of rulers with common heritage.

famine Widespread starvation due to insufficient crop production.

figurine A small statue, statuette.

hieroglyph A symbol or picture that represents a concept.

mummify The process of preserving the bodies of the dead through a certain type of embalmment.

myth A morality tale that was passed along in ancient times.

Nile The longest river in the world, which passes through Egypt.

papyrus A type of paper made from a water plant that was used for writing in ancient Egypt.

pharaoh An ancient Egyptian ruler.

pyramids Monumental tombs built for the ancient Egyptian pharaohs.

ritual A preplanned and repeated process.

scribe A person who copied documents in ancient times.

sphinx An ancient Egyptian stone figure with the body of a lion and head of a human or animal.

tomb A burial place, notably for rulers in ancient Egypt.

FOR MORE INFORMATION

American Museum of Natural History
Central Park West at 79th Street
New York, NY 10024-5192
(800) 462-8687
Web site: http://www.amnh.org
The American Museum of Natural History in New York offers exhibitions on many ancient societies, including that of Egypt.

Ancient Egypt for Kids
Kidipede
2007 NE 25th Avenue
Portland, OR 97212
(800) 280-4132 x704
Web site: http://www.historyforkids.org/learn/egypt
The Kidipede Ancient Egypt exhibition offers insightful information on the history and culture of ancient Egypt.

Egyptian Museum
Midan El Tahrir
Cairo, Egypt 11557
(202) 578-2448
Web site: http://www.egyptianmuseum.gov.eg

The Egyptian Museum, located in Cairo, Egypt, was founded in 1835 by the Egyptian government and offers rich information about the history and culture of ancient Egypt.

Penn Museum
A New Look at Ancient Egypt
3260 South Street
Philadelphia, PA 19104
(215) 898-4000
Web site: http://www.museum.upenn.edu
The Penn Museum's "A New Look at Ancient Egypt" exhibit offers displays of relics and other archaeological remains from ancient Egypt.

Web Sites

Due to the changing nature of Internet links, Rosen Publishing has developed an online list of Web sites related to the subject of this book. This site is updated regularly. Please use this link to access the list:

http://www.rosenlinks.com/anc/egypt

FOR FURTHER READING

Brewer, Douglas J. and Emily Teeter. *Egypt and the Egyptians*. New York, NY: Cambridge University Press, 2007.

Dodson, Aidan. *The Complete Royal Families of Ancient Egypt: A Genealogical Sourcebook of the Pharaohs*. New York, NY: Thames & Hudson, 2004.

Perl, Lila. *The Ancient Egyptians* (People of the Ancient World). New York, NY: Children's Press, 2005.

Pinch, Geraldine. *Egyptian Mythology: A Guide to the Gods, Goddesses, and Traditions of Ancient Egypt*. New York, NY: Oxford University Press, 2004.

Robins, Gay. *The Art of Ancient Egypt*. Cambridge, MA: Harvard University Press, 2000.

Tyldesley, Joyce A. *Chronicle of the Queens of Egypt*. New York, NY: Thames & Hudson, 2006.

Tyldesley, Joyce A. *Nefertiti: Unlocking the Mystery Surrounding Egypt's Most Famous and Beautiful Queen*. New York, NY: Penguin, 2005.

Wilkinson, Richard H. *The Complete Gods and Goddesses of Ancient Egypt*. New York, NY: Thames & Hudson, 2003.

Wilkinson, Toby. *Lives of the Ancient Egyptians: Pharaohs, Queens, Courtiers and Commoners*. New York, NY: Thames & Hudson, 2007.

INDEX

A

afterlife, 13, 16, 22, 25, 38
Amun-Ra (god), 6, 8, 14
Anubis (god), 13, 16, 38
Atef (crown), 20

B

Ba, 12
Bastet (goddess), 42
Bes (god), 13
Book of the Dead, 12, 25
burial customs, 9, 13, 16, 17

C

canopic jars, 16
Champollion, Jean François, 25
clothes, 12, 20, 28, 33, 36
Coffin Texts, 25
crowns, 8, 9, 20, 37

D

Deir el-Medina, 25, 33
Delta, 8, 24
Demotic script, 24, 25
Denderah, 13
Deshret (crown), 8, 20, 37
Diodorus, 41

E

Egyptian calendar, 9
Euphrates, River, 36

F

farming, 9, 13, 28, 38, 40
Fayum lake, 41
First Intermediate Period, 25
fishing, 38, 40, 41
food, 13, 32, 38, 40, 41

G

Geb (god), 6, 8
Giza, 17
grave goods, 9, 13, 32
Great Pyramid, 17
Great Royal Wife, 21

H

Hapy (god), 9
Hathor (goddess), 13, 22, 29, 42
Hedjet (crown), 8, 20
hieratic script, 24
hieroglyphics, 9, 24, 25, 43
hippopotamus, 18, 19, 38, 41, 43
Hittites, 21, 36, 37
Horus (god), 10, 13, 18, 19, 20, 29
houses, 33
hunting, 38, 40, 41, 43

I

Imhotep, (architect) 17, 20
Isis (goddess), 10, 13, 18, 29

J

Judgement of the Soul, 38

K

Ka, 12, 13
Khephri, 14
Khnum (god), 6, 11

L

Lotus, 6, 12, 26
Lower Egypt, 8, 10, 20, 37, 42
Luxor, 33

M

Maat (goddess), 16, 21
marriage, 28, 29

Mediterranean Sea, 8, 36
Memphis, 8
Middle Kingdom, 25, 41
mummies, 5, 13, 16, 36, 42, 43
Muwatallis, King, 37

N

Narmer Palette, 8, 37
Nefertiti, Queen, 21, 29
Nekhbet (goddess), 42
Nephthys (goddess), 6
New Kingdom, 25, 32, 36, 37
Nile, River, 6, 8, 9, 10, 18, 33, 38, 40, 41, 42, 43
Nile Valley, 8
Nilometers, 9
Nubia, 22, 36, 37
Nut (goddess), 6, 8

O

Old Kingdom, 25, 41, 42
Opening of the Mouth, 16
Orontes, River, 37
Osiris (god), 6, 10, 13, 19, 20, 25, 29, 38, 41, 43

P

Palestine, 36, 40
papyrus, 12, 24, 25, 36, 42, 43
pharaohs, 5, 12, 16, 17, 20, 21, 29, 34, 35, 36, 37, 41, 42
   Akhenaten, 21, 29
   Amenhophis III, 37
   Cheops, 16, 17
   Chephren, 20
   Djoser, 17
   Menes or Narmer, 8
   Ptolemy II Philadelphus, 43
   Ramesses II, 21, 36, 37
   Snefru, 17, 26, 27

48

Thutmose III, 36
Tutankhamen, 21
Predynastic burials, 9
Predynastic Egypt, 8, 9
priests, 12, 13, 20, 21, 26, 31, 40
Pschent (crown), 20
Ptah (god), 20, 42
Punt, 34, 36
Pyramid Texts, 25
pyramids, 5, 6, 16, 17, 25, 41

Q

Qadesh, Battle of, 37
Queens, 21, 32

R

Ra (god), 17, 22, 43
Rosetta Stone, 25

S

Saqqara, 17, 42
scribes, 20, 22, 24, 25, 40, 42, 43
Second Intermediate Period, 25
Selket (goddess), 42
Seth (god), 6, 10, 18, 19, 41
Seven Wonders of the Ancient World, 16
shaduf, 41
Shu (god), 6, 8
Sobek (god), 42
Sphinx, the, 5, 17
Syria, 36, 37, 40

T

temples, 12, 13, 20, 21, 37, 40
Thebes, 21, 40

Thoth (god), 13, 16, 22, 24, 30, 31
trade, 36, 40

U

Underworld, the, 10, 14, 16, 19, 20
Upper Egypt, 8, 9, 20, 42

V

Valley of the Kings, 21
vizier, 20

W

Wadjet (goddess), 40
warfare, 36, 37
weapons, 9, 36
Weighing of the Heart, 16
women, 13, 25, 28, 29, 32